WRITE RIGHT!

WRITE RIGHT!
A Canadian desk-drawer digest of punctuation, grammar, and style

Jan Venolia

International Self-Counsel Press Ltd.
Head and Editorial Office
Vancouver
Toronto   Seattle

Printed in Canada
First edition: October, 1980
Second edition: April, 1983
Reprinted: June, 1985

Cataloguing in Publication Data
Venolia, Jan, 1928-
     Write right!

     (Self-counsel series)
     Bibliography: p.
     Includes index.
     ISBN 0-88908-554-4

     1. English language - Grammar - 1950-
     2. English language - Punctuation.   I. Title.
     II. Series.
     PE1112.V4 1980   808'.042   C80-091240-3

A U.S. edition of this book has been published by Ten Speed Press.

International Self-Counsel Press Ltd.
Head and Editorial Office
306 West 25th Street
North Vancouver, British Columbia V7N 2G1
Vancouver   Toronto   Seattle

Table of Contents

Read this first:

Write Right! has grown from two observations I made during my ten years as a freelance writer and editor: Certain types of grammatical errors occur repeatedly, and improvement in those areas alone markedly improves the quality of writing.

The need for help with these troublesome points of grammar and punctuation has been expressed by most of my clients or their secretaries. I referred them to the best books I knew on the subject, but felt that even the best were either too limited or too complicated to be useful as desk references. Eventually I realized that the best way to get a book that met their needs was to write one. This is it.

My philosophy has been to provide a combination first-aid kit and preventive maintenance manual for the written word. I selected all of the subject matter with an eye to its being most useful most often to most people. Thus you will find that I did not include all punctuation marks. I could not think of an important use of the period, for example, that would not be obvious to any user of this book. Similarly, I assumed anyone consulting this book will know that most sentences start with a capital letter and end with a period and that they will not be concerned with such academic refinements as syllepsis, zeugma, or hysteron proteron.

Write Right! lands between the elementary and the exotic. Its aim is not to delve into the fine points of English grammar and punctuation, but to simplify some of the most important ones so that they become accessible for everyday use. Wherever possible, I have used quotations from noted individuals to illustrate the rules since Mark Twain is more entertaining than a primer-style sentence. But don't lose sight of the fact that each quotation is there to illustrate the preceding rule.

1

I suggest that you skim through the pages to become familiar with what is covered. The examples provided, together with the glossary in the back of the book, will help you understand any rule whose application is not immediately obvious. In some cases, the glossary provides all the explanation that seems necessary for a given topic; for example, split infinitives are covered only in the glossary because they are no longer considered to be important grammatically.

Possibly one of the most helpful sections in the book is a list of words that are frequently confused or abused. There you can learn at a glance whether you should use *farther* or *further*, *bi-* or *semi-*, *who* or *whom*. The correct choice in such matters bears directly on the professional appearance of your writing.

If you have a knotty problem that is not covered within these pages, one of the books listed in the bibliography will probably help. A good dictionary is a must. It not only tells you how to spell a word and where to divide it, but frequently also provides examples that help you determine correct usage. Several dictionaries are listed in the bibliography.

Written communications are an increasingly important element of our lives. By improving the quality of our writing, we improve our chances of being understood.

> *Unless one is a genius, it is best to aim at being intelligible.*
> — Anthony Hope

Punctuation Pointers

PUNCTUATION POINTERS

Properly used punctuation helps the reader understand the writer. It indicates when to pause, which items belong together, whether something is omitted, or what is being emphasized. Misused punctuation, on the other hand, can mislead, distort meaning, and interrupt the flow of ideas.

Many of the choices regarding punctuation are determined by what the writer wants to say or emphasize. Keep in mind that the goal is to help the reader understand your meaning, and many of your choices will become automatic.

When you find a sentence particularly hard to punctuate, the problem may not be punctuation but writing style. Rewriting a basically flawed sentence may be your best alternative.

THE APOSTROPHE

1. Use an apostrophe to indicate possession:

a) with nouns (both singular and plural) that do not end with the letter *s*, add an apostrophe and *s*;

women's rights   children's hour

Canada's climate is nine months winter and three months late fall. — Evan Esar

Some people's money is merited, and other people's is inherited. — Ogden Nash

b) with *plural* nouns that end with *s*, add only an apostrophe;

the Joneses' dog   the flight attendants' duties

5

c) with *singular* nouns that end with *s*, add either the apostrophe alone *or* both the apostrophe and *s*, depending on which authority you choose to go by.

William Strunk, Jr., author of *The Elements of Style*, insists that all singular possessives are formed by adding *'s*, regardless of the final consonant. Thus:

Charles's hat   Marx's theories
John Jones's dog   the witness's testimony

The exceptions he allows are ancient proper names (Jesus' robe, Achilles' heel) and such constructions as *for goodness' sake*. On the other hand, some authorities state that singular possessives with words ending in *s* are formed by adding only an apostrophe. Still others indicate that if a *sis* or *siz* sound is desired when a singular noun ends in *s*, both apostrophe and *s* are added. Thus you would be correct in saying either *Dickens' novels* or *Dickens's novels*, depending on which rule you chose as your guide. In no case, however, would you be correct in writing *Dicken's novels*, since the author's name was not *Dicken*.

In some expressions the idea of possession no longer seems to apply, and the apostrophe has been dropped. These words are then considered adjectives that modify the accompanying noun.

Teachers College   two weeks vacation   Teamsters Union

NOTE: With the exception of the word *one's*, possessive pronouns *(its, hers, his, theirs, yours, ours, whose)* never have an apostrophe — they already show possession.

The dog wagged its tail (not *it's* tail).

The speaker whose tie has gravy on it (not *who's* tie)...

The mistake of adding an apostrophe to the already possessive pronoun *its* is particularly common. Remember that an apostrophe in the word *it's* indicates a contraction of *it is*.

It's not easy to put the apostrophe in its place.

6

d) If possession is common to two or more individuals, only the last name takes the apostrophe.

Tom and Dick's boat (*not* Tom's and Dick's boat)

But if possession is not common, make each noun possessive.

men's, women's, and children's apparel

(See Rule 57d regarding possessives of compound words.)

2. Use an apostrophe in contractions to indicate omission of letters or numbers.

summer of '42, can't, won't, he's, they're, isn't, it's, etc.

Pleasure's a sin, and sometimes sin's a pleasure. — Lord Byron

I'm not denyin' the women are foolish: God Almighty made 'em to match the men. — George Eliot

Most contractions are not appropriate in formal writing, but they should be used when avoiding them results in stilted or awkward sentences. If you have any doubts about a contraction, try saying the complete words without the contraction to see if the words make sense.

you're sure (you are sure, *not* your sure)

you're welcome (you are welcome, *not* your welcome)

This precaution will avoid, for example, the common misuse of the word *there's*. Many people might say or write *there's differences* when they wouldn't dream of saying *there* **is** *differences*.

7

3. Use an apostrophe with nouns that are followed by a gerund (see Glossary for definition of gerund).

> The plane's leaving on time amazed us all.

> Six weeks in a cast was the result of Donna's skiing.

4. Use an apostrophe in the following cases:

—to form plurals of abbreviations that have periods

> M.D.'s

—with letters where addition of *s* alone would be confusing

> p's and q's

—and with words used merely as words without regard to their meaning.

> Don't give me any *if's, and's,* or *but's.*

THE COLON

5. Use a colon before a list, summary, long quotation, or final clause that explains or amplifies preceding matter.

> *There are three kinds of lies: lies, damned lies, and statistics.*
> — Disraeli

> *There are two reasons for drinking: one is, when you are thirsty, to cure it; the other, when you are not thirsty, to prevent it.*
> — Thomas Peacock

A wise statesman once said: The art of taxation consists in so plucking the goose as to obtain the largest amount of feathers with the least possible amount of hissing.

Marriage may be compared to a cage: The birds outside despair to get in and those within despair to get out. — Montaigne

(See Rule 48 regarding capitalization of the first word following a colon.)

6. **Use a colon following a phrase in which the words** *as follows* **or** *the following* **are either expressed or implied.**

General Nathan Forrest had the following prescription for victory: "Git thar fustest with the mostest."

The ingredients of a diplomat's life have been identified as follows: protocol, alcohol, and Geritol.

Many hazards await the unwary consumer: deceptive packaging, misleading labels, and shoddy workmanship.

NOTE: Do not use a colon when the items of a list come immediately after a verb or preposition:

Wrong: The job requirements are: typing, shorthand, and bookkeeping.

Right: The job requirements are typing, shorthand, and bookkeeping.

THE COMMA

7. Use a comma in a sentence that contains two complete statements (independent clauses) that are joined by the conjunctions *but, nor,* or *for*.

> *Soap and education are not as sudden as a massacre, but they are more deadly in the long run.* — Mark Twain

> *It is always a silly thing to give advice, but to give good advice is absolutely fatal.* — Oscar Wilde

a) The comma is optional when two independent clauses are joined by the conjunctions *and* or *or*.

> *A little sincerity is a dangerous thing, and a great deal of it is absolutely fatal.* — Oscar Wilde

> *Give a little love to a child and you get a great deal back.* — John Ruskin

The comma is omitted if the statements are short and closely related.

> *The wise make proverbs and fools repeat them.* — Isaac D'Israeli

> *Power tends to corrupt and absolute power corrupts absolutely.* — Lord Acton

---

NOTE: Do not use a comma before *and* or *or* unless there is a complete statement on each side of the conjunction.

Wrong: I resented his interference, and her superior smile.
(*her superior smile* is not a complete statement)

Right: *The optimist proclaims that we live in the best of all possible worlds, and the pessimist fears this is true.* — James Branch Cabell

---

b) **Do not use a comma between an independent and a dependent clause.** (Dependent clauses are incomplete statements that could not stand alone; the dependent clauses in the following examples are underlined.)

Facts do not cease to exist because they are ignored.
— Aldous Huxley

A fanatic is one who can't change his mind and won't change the subject. — Attr. to Winston Churchill

The art of medicine consists of amusing the patient while nature cures the disease. — Voltaire

Old age isn't so bad when you consider the alternative.
— Maurice Chevalier

8. Use commas between the elements of a series of three or more words, phrases, or clauses.

Eat, drink, and be leery. — O. Henry

After three days men grow weary of a wench, a guest, and rainy weather. — Benjamin Franklin

---

NOTE: The final comma in a series is optional. However, I prefer to use a comma before the conjunction joining the last two items because it gives equal weight to each of the items and avoids confusion. The following example with the final comma omitted illustrates my point:

Clean sheets, the smell of freshly baked bread and my kid sister all remind me of home.

Whichever style you choose, with or without a final comma, use it consistently.

11

9. Use commas between consecutive adjectives where the comma is essentially being used instead of the word *and*.

the tall, dark, handsome man   a ripe, juicy apple

An experienced, industrious, ambitious, and often quite picturesque liar. — Mark Twain

Do not use a comma between consecutive adjectives if the first adjective modifies the idea expressed by the second adjective and the noun combined.

tall brick wall   noisy time clock   cold roast beef
(adj.)(adj.+noun)

An easy way to determine if an adjective modifies only the noun instead of the combination of the second adjective and the noun is to see if you can plausibly insert the word *and* between the two adjectives. *Ripe and juicy apple* sounds acceptable, and thus use of a comma would be appropriate. But you wouldn't be inclined to say *cold and roast beef*, hence no commas.

Still another way to test whether a comma is called for is to reverse the order of the adjectives. When the sequence of the adjectives is reversible, as in *juicy, ripe apple*, a comma should be used. When the sequence cannot be reversed, no comma is used (as in *cold roast beef*).

10. Use commas to set off certain phrases and clauses.

a) indicating contrast (antithetical phrases)

Virtue consists, not in abstaining from vice, but in not desiring it.
— G. B. Shaw

Advice is judged by results, not by intentions. — Cicero

The fool wonders, the wise man asks. — Benjamin Disraeli

b) parenthetical phrases (as if contained in parentheses)

Pessimism, when you get used to it, is just as agreeable as optimism.
— Arnold Bennett

Great blunders are often made, like large ropes, of a multitude of fibers. — Victor Hugo

Silence, it has been said by one writer, is a virtue which renders us agreeable to our fellow creatures. — Samuel Butler

> *NOTE:* In sentences such as the above, be sure to use a *pair* of commas around the parenthetical phrase.

c) appositive phrases
(Appositives are nouns or phrases that are placed next to a word to provide identification or additional information.)

Marshall McLuhan, author of *The Medium is the Massage,* calls language a form of organized stutter.

Stuart Keate, former publisher of the *Vancouver Sun,* once wrote that Canada is the vichyssoise of nations — cold, half-French, and difficult to stir.

d) descriptive phrases or clauses that are nonrestrictive
(Nonrestrictive phrases add information that is not essential to the meaning of the sentence or necessary for identification.)

My daughter, who is a pilot, enjoys classical music.

The above example is punctuated correctly if the writer has only one daughter. But if the writer has more than one daughter, the phrase *who is a pilot* is essential for identification, and the commas must be omitted.

13

The underlined phrases in the following examples are restrictive (i.e., they tell *which* life, *which* hand, or *which* person) — thus, no commas are appropriate. Notice how omission of the restrictive phrases would distort the meaning of the sentences or leave them meaningless.

> *The life <u>which is unexamined</u> is not worth living.* — Plato

> *The hand <u>that rocks the cradle</u> is the hand <u>that rules the world</u>.*
> — William Wallace

> *A Canadian is somebody <u>who knows how to make love in a canoe</u>.* — Pierre Berton

e) introductory words, phrases, or clauses

> *In general, the art of government consists in taking as much money as possible from one class of citizens to give to the other.*
> — Voltaire
> *When angry, count four; when very angry, swear.* — Mark Twain
>
> *Meanwhile, the meek are a long time inheriting the earth.*
> — Bob Edwards

In the following examples, commas have been omitted to demonstrate how helpful they can be to the reader.

> As discussed earlier discharges were highly toxic.

> Ever since John has regretted his decision.

> After eating the tigers dozed off.

Insert the commas correctly, and you will save the reader having to read the sentences twice.

f) dependent clauses that precede the main clause

> *As scarce as truth is, the supply has always been in excess of demand.*
> — Josh Billings

14

If fifty million people say a foolish thing, it is still a foolish thing.
— Anatole France

Though familiarity may not breed contempt, it takes the edge off admiration. — William Hazlitt

If at first you don't succeed, don't take any more chances.
— Kin Hubbard

11. Use a comma between words that demand a pause or might otherwise be misunderstood.

Whatever you do, do well.

To Ross, Hunter remained insulting.

Out of sight, out of mind.

12. Use a comma to set off a direct address.

No, Agnes, a Bordeaux is not a house of ill-repute.
— George Bain

To lose one parent, Mr. Worthing, may be regarded as a misfortune; to lose both looks like carelessness. — Oscar Wilde

13. Use a comma to set off a direct quotation from the rest of the sentence.

Admiral Farragut said, "Damn the torpedoes!"

"Take some more tea," the March Hare said to Alice, very earnestly. "I've had nothing yet," Alice replied in an offended tone, "so I can't take more." "You mean you can't take less," said the Hatter. "It's very easy to take more than nothing."
— Lewis Carroll

(See Rule 36 regarding other punctuation of quotations.)

15

14. Use a comma to indicate omission of a word or words.

> *A man likes you for what he thinks you are; a woman, for what you think she is.* — Ivan Panin

(The phrase *likes you* is omitted from the second half of the sentence.)

> *It takes little talent to see clearly what lies under one's nose, a good deal of it to know in which direction to point that organ.*
> — W. H. Auden

> *When angry, count ten before you speak; if very angry, a hundred.*
> — Thomas Jefferson

15. Use a comma following the words *for example, that is, namely,* **and their abbreviations** (*e.g., i.e., viz.*). Punctuation preceding these words depends on the strength of the pause you desire.

> One era's artifacts become another's source of antiques; for example, moustache cups and chamberpots.

> A liking for the primary colors (i.e., red, yellow, and blue) is considered a sign of mental health.

16. The comma following conjunctive adverbs (such as *accordingly, furthermore, however, therefore, thus, indeed, nevertheless,* and *consequently*) **is optional, depending on whether you wish to indicate a pause.**

> Sales have dropped precipitously; furthermore, employee morale has reached a new low.

> Grammar books frequently do not explain rules of usage so they can be understood; indeed they are sometimes entirely useless!

> *I think I think; therefore, I think I am.* — Ambrose Bierce

> *Any man's death diminishes me, because I am involved in Mankind; and therefore never send to know for whom the bell tolls, it tolls for thee.* — John Donne

16

17. Where *not* to use the comma.

Although commas can help the reader understand your meaning, a sentence that is overloaded with commas creates a choppy, abrasive effect that slows down and antagonizes the reader. As with all punctuation marks, if you use commas sparingly and correctly, you will find that you are using them effectively.

Here are some places where commas do *not* belong:

a) Do not use a comma between two independent clauses unless they are joined by a conjunction.

Wrong: The Dow Jones Industrial Average hit a new high, the dollar continued to climb in foreign markets.

This error is called a *comma fault*, because the writer is asking too much of the comma, using it where a stronger punctuation mark (period, semicolon) is required. (See Glossary.)

Remember that independent clauses are complete within themselves and could stand as separate sentences. Unless they are joined by a conjunction (*and, but, or, nor, for,* etc.) they must either be separated by a semicolon or written as two sentences.

Wrong: The product was an in-house success, it simply didn't sell.

Right: The product was an in-house success; it simply didn't sell.
The product was an in-house success. It simply didn't sell.

b) Do not separate subject and verb by a comma.

This error frequently occurs when a comma is placed *following* the last item in a series, as in the following example:

Wrong: Riding motorcycles, hang-gliding, and skydiving, were the main pastimes in her short life.

or when the subject is a phrase:

Wrong: Placing a comma between subject and verb, is incorrect.

THE DASH

18. Use the dash for emphasis, to indicate an abrupt change, or with explanatory phrases or words (in place of commas or parentheses).

Scenery is fine — but human nature is finer. — John Keats.

Money is like a sixth sense—and you can't make use of the other five without it. — Somerset Maugham

It takes two to speak the truth—one to speak, and another to hear. — Thoreau

---

NOTE: Be sure to use dashes both before and after a phrase when it is in the middle of a sentence, not a dash before the phrase and a comma after it.

All our lives we are putting pennies—our most Golden Pennies—into penny-in-the-slot machines that are empty. — Logan Pearsall Smith

---

Avoid routinely using the dash in place of commas. By overuse, you lose the effectiveness of this punctuation mark.

THE ELLIPSIS

19. Use an ellipsis to indicate an omission within a quotation. Ellipses consist of three spaced periods (i.e., a space before each period and after the last).

We are told that talent creates its own opportunities. But . . . intense desire creates not only its own opportunities, but its own talents. — Eric Hoffer

Despite my thirty years of research into the feminine soul, I have not yet been able to answer . . . the great question . . . What does a woman want? — Sigmund Freud

THE HYPHEN

20. Use a hyphen with certain prefixes and suffixes.
   a) to avoid doubling or tripling a letter

   re-evaluate   anti-intellectual
   shell-like   pre-empt

   b) if the root word begins with a capital letter

   un-American   anti-Israeli
   pre-Christmas   post-World War II

   c) in general, with the prefixes *all-, ex-, self-, vice-,* **and with the suffix** *-elect*

   all-knowing   self-made
   ex-husband   vice-president
   president-elect   all-purpose

   Self-sacrifice enables us to sacrifice other people without blushing.
   — G. B. Shaw

   d) to avoid awkward pronunciations or ambiguity

   un-ionized   anti-nuclear
   co-worker   re-read

21. Use a hyphen after a series of words having a common base that is not repeated.

   first-, second-, and third-basemen

   small- and middle-sized companies

19

22. Use a hyphen to form certain compound words.

(Compound words unite two or more words, with or without a hyphen, to convey a single idea.)

The current trend is to write compound words as one word (e.g., handgun, airborne, turnkey, stockbroker). However, the hyphen should be retained in the following cases:

a) in compound nouns, where needed for clarity or as an aid in pronunciation

right-of-way	editor-in-chief
sit-in	come-on

The awe and dread with which the untutored savage contemplates his mother-in-law are amongst the most familiar facts of anthropology. — Sir James Frazier

b) in compound adjectives (unit modifiers) when they precede the word they modify

well-to-do individual	solid-state circuit
matter-of-fact statement	twentieth-century dilemma
well-designed unit	up-to-date accounting methods

The authors adopted an I-can-laugh-at-it-now-but-it-was-no-laughing-matter-at-the-time attitude. — Theodore Bernstein

If the words that make up the compound adjectives in the above examples *follow* the words they modify, they are no longer compound adjectives, and no hyphens are used.

The unit is well designed.

Their accounting methods are up to date.

NOTE: If each of the adjectives could modify the noun without the other adjective, more than a single thought is involved (i.e., it is not a compound adjective), and a hyphen is not used.

a happy, healthy child   a new digital alarm clock

---

c) with improvised compounds

know-it-all	stick-in-the-mud
Johnny-come-lately	do-it-yourselfer

He spoke with a certain what-is-it in his voice, and I could see that if not actually disgruntled, he was far from being gruntled.
— P. G. Wodehouse

The *Style Book* prepared by the Canadian Press has a helpful list that indicates whether compound words should be written as one word, two words, or hyphenated.

NOTE: Never form a hyphenated compound with a word ending in *-ly*.

newly formed company	widely known facts

---

23. **Use a hyphen in fractions and compound numbers from 21 to 99.**

three-fourths	thirty-seven
one-third	forty-two

24. **Use a hyphen to combine numeral-unit adjectives.**

12-inch ruler	5-cent cigar
30-day month	100-year lifespan

25. **Use a hyphen to combine an initial capital letter with a word.**

T-shirt	X-rated
U-turn	V-neck

26. **Use a hyphen to divide a word at the right-hand margin.** (See Rules 62-64).

(See Rule 49b regarding capitalization of hyphenated words.)

21

PARENTHESES

Parentheses seldom present a problem in writing, but the punctuation surrounding them frequently does. You should use parentheses primarily when you want to de-emphasize some explanatory matter (in contrast with dashes, which draw attention to the elements they set off).

27. **Enclose the punctuation associated with complete statements within the parentheses.**

> (How I wish he would!)

> (Events later confirmed his suspicions.)

28. **When a parenthetical item falls in the middle of a sentence, punctuation needed at that point** *follows* **the closing parenthesis.**

> There is only one problem (and he admits it): his chronic tardiness.

In other words, do not put a comma, semicolon, colon, or dash before an opening parenthesis.

Wrong: I phoned him when I arrived, (as I had promised) but he was not at home.

Right: I phoned him when I arrived (as I had promised), but he was not at home.

29. **When a parenthesis falls at the end of a sentence, the closing punctuation follows the final parenthesis.**

> I phoned him when I arrived (as I had promised).

22

THE QUESTION MARK

30. A question mark is used at the end of a question. That much is obvious. But whether question marks are needed at the end of every request is not always clear. A good general rule is that if the reader is expected to act instead of reply, no question mark is necessary. But if you feel the request is too presumptuous as a statement, use a question mark.

> Will you please send me a one-year subscription.
> Will you please feed the cat while I'm away?

QUOTATION MARKS

31. Use quotation marks for a direct quotation (i.e. the exact words),

> *"I'm world-famous,"* Dr. Parks said, *"all over Canada."*
> — Mordecai Richler

but not an indirect one (i.e., a rearrangement or restatement of the person's words).

> Pascal said that most of the disorders and evils in life are the result of man's inability to sit still and think.

32. Use quotation marks to enclose a word or phrase that is defined.

> The word "ventana" is Spanish for window.
>
> "Qualifying small businesses" means those with fewer than 250 employees.

33. Use quotation marks to enclose words or phrases following such terms as *entitled, the word(s), the term, marked, designated, classified, named, endorsed,* **or** *signed.*

> The cheque was endorsed "John Hancock."
> *The word "impossible" is not in my dictionary.* — Napoleon

23

34. Use quotation marks to indicate a misnomer or special meaning for a word.

Some "antiques" would more accurately be described as junk.

A "brass hat" is an officer of at least one rank higher than you whom you don't like and who doesn't like you. — Kenneth Royall

It is easy to overdo this usage, resulting in a cloying, affected style.

> *NOTE:* Do not use quotation marks following the words *known as, called, so-called,* etc. unless the expressions that follow are misnomers or slang.
>
> *Most of the luxuries, and many of the so-called comforts, of life are not only not indispensable, but positive hindrances to the elevation of mankind.* — Thoreau

35. Use quotation marks to enclose titles of *component parts* of whole publications: chapters or other divisions of a book; articles in periodicals; songs; stories, essays, poems, and the like, in anthologies or similar collections.

Titles of *whole* published works such as books, periodicals, plays, and reports should be underlined or italicized.

36. Punctuation with quotation marks.

Punctuation associated with quotation marks is sometimes more troublesome than the quotation marks themselves. Here is the best rule:

Comma and final period are placed *inside* the quotation marks. Other punctuation marks are placed *outside* the quotation marks unless they are part of the material being quoted.

He shouted, "All aboard!"

She had the audacity to answer "No"!

Who asked "Why?"

Do you think we should watch "News Hour"?

Charts answer the question "how much," maps answer the question "where," and diagrams answer the question "how."

"My country, right or wrong" is like saying "My mother, drunk or sober." — G. K. Chesterton

37. **Use single quotation marks to indicate a quote within a quote.**

Kin Hubbard wrote: "When a fellow says, 'It ain't the money but the principle of the thing,' it's the money."

THE SEMICOLON

38. **Use a semicolon between independent clauses that are too closely related to be written as separate sentences.**

Children begin by loving their parents; as they grow older they judge them; sometimes they forgive them. — Oscar Wilde

It is with narrow-souled people as with narrow-necked bottles; the less they have in them, the more noise they make in pouring out. — Alexander Pope

A neurotic is the man who builds a castle in the air; a psychotic is the man who lives in it; and a psychiatrist is the man who collects the rent. — Lord Webb-Johnson

39. **Use a semicolon to separate a series of phrases that already contain commas.**

The meeting was attended by Lloyd Harrison, president of the board; Evelyn White, chief delegate of the consumer groups; William Blake, representing the press; and Preston Tracy, speaking for the shareholders.

40. **Use a semicolon preceding explanatory phrases introduced by words such as *for example, that is,* or *namely* when you want a stronger break than a comma would provide.**

Secretaries have many unpopular assignments; for example, making coffee.

41. Use a semicolon between independent clauses that are long or contain commas.

Susan returned yesterday from her trip to Europe, according to her mother; and on her arrival at the airport, she was met by her entire family.

Doing business without advertising is like winking at a girl in the dark; you know what you are doing, but nobody else does. — S. Britt

---

NOTE: The conjunctive adverb *however* seems to invite punctuation errors. In fact, incorrect punctuation surrounding the word *however* is one of the two most frequent errors I encounter in my editing assignments (the other is the use of *it's* as a possessive pronoun; see Note, p. 6). The difficulty appears to be the assumption that *however* and a pair of commas are sufficient to glue together two independent clauses. Instead, the result is a *comma fault.* (See Glossary.)

Wrong: Projections were gloomy, however, sales skyrocketed.

Two independent clauses joined by *however* require a complete stop (either a semicolon or a period).

Right: Projections were gloomy; however, sales skyrocketed.

A comma follows *however* whenever it is an interruption or suggests contrast with something preceding it—which is most of the time. But when *however* is used in the sense of "no matter how," no comma is used.

Let him step to the music which he hears, however measured or far away. — Thoreau

---

26

Mechanics

MECHANICS

ABBREVIATIONS

A good rule of thumb for formal writing is *Don't abbrev*. However, when abbreviations are appropriate, as in company names, military titles, outside addresses, and footnotes, be sure to use them correctly.

42. **The preferred abbreviation for a province (or a state) in an outside address is two capital letters and no period.**

Alberta AB	Nova Scotia NS
British Columbia BC	Ontario ON
Manitoba MB	Prince Edward Island PE
New Brunswick NB	Quebec PQ
Newfoundland NF	Saskatchewan SK
Northwest Territories NT	Yukon YT

Do not abbreviate inside addresses (i.e., those typed on the first page of the letter).

43. **You may abbreviate titles only when you use the person's full name.**

Gen. Frances Fyte

Rev. Sam Soule

If the full name is not used, do not abbreviate any titles (General Fyte, *not* Gen. Fyte). Similarly, a full date can be abbreviated (Dec. 7, 1941), but a partial date should be written in full (December 7, *not* Dec. 7).

44. The correct (formal) plural of the abbreviation *Mr.* is *Messrs.*, and of *Mrs.* is *Mmes.*

    Ms. seems to be replacing *Miss* or *Mrs.* and can be useful when you don't know a woman's marital status.

45. When an abbreviated word is also a contraction, do not use an apostrophe to indicate the contraction.

    Intl., *not* Int'l. (for *International*)

46. Use an apostrophe to form the plural of an abbreviation that has periods.

    Seventy-three M.D.'s attended the meeting.

47. Abbreviations frequently used in footnotes include:

    p. (page)
    pp. (pages)
    ibid. (*ibidem*, in the same place)
    ca. (*circa*, about; usually used to indicate an approximate date)
    cf. (compare)

CAPITALIZATION

48. Capitalize the first word after a colon if it begins a complete statement.

    In summary: The evidence has proved a clear case of murder.

    My final point: Keeping your nose to the grindstone and your shoulder to the wheel will produce curvature of the spine.

    That man must be tremendously ignorant: He answers every question that is put to him. — Voltaire

49. Capitalize titles as follows:

a) In titles of books, plays, television programs, etc., capitalize the first and last words, plus all principal words.
Articles, conjunctions, and short prepositions are not capitalized unless they begin the title. Prepositions are capitalized if they consist of four or more letters or if they are connected with a preceding verb.

> Stop the World, I Want to Get Off
>
> Customers Held Up by Gunmen
>
> Situation Calls For Action

b) Capitalize both parts of a hyphenated word in a title unless it is considered as one word or is a compound numeral.

> Report of the Ninety-fifth Parliament
> Well-Known Author Dies
> Anti-inflation Measures Taken

c) Personal titles are capitalized only if they precede the name and are not separated by a comma.

> Professor Reynolds
> the treasurer, Will Knott

Capitalization is optional if the title follows the noun.

> Lightfoot Walker, president of the corporation
> *or* Lightfoot Walker, President of the corporation.

50. Capitalize both the full names and the shortened names of government agencies, bureaus, departments, services, etc.

> Parks Branch
> Sheriff's Office
> Statistics Canada
> Bureau of Pension Advocates
> Ombudsman of B.C.
> Law Reform Commission

Do not capitalize the words *government, federal, administration,* etc. except when part of the title of a specific entity.

> The Canadian Government is the largest employer in the nation.

> She hopes to work for the federal government.

Capitalization of departments or divisions of a company is optional.

> Claims Department, *or* claims department
> Engineering Division, *or* engineering division

51. Capitalize points of the compass and regional terms when they refer to specific sections or when they are part of a precise descriptive title,

> the East   Vancouver's West End
> the Western Hemisphere   Eastern Europe

but not when merely suggesting direction or position.

> western provinces   south of town
> east coast   northern lights

> *Go west, young man.* —John B. L. Soule

Some regional terms, such as *Prairie Provinces,* seem to be either part of a "precise descriptive title" or "merely suggest position," depending on your viewpoint. Since authorities can be found on both sides of this gray area, I suggest you choose whichever you are more comfortable with, and capitalize accordingly.

32

52. Capitalize abbreviations, if the words they stand for are capitalized.

M.D.	M.P.
Ph.D.	M.L.A.

53. Capitalize ethnic groups, factions, alliances, and political parties, but not the word *party*, itself.

He spoke for the Chinese community.

The Liberal party held its convention in July.

The Communist bloc vetoed the proposal.

NOTE: Political groupings other than parties are usually lowercased:

He represents the left wing of the Canadian Labor Congress.

But:

the Right, the Left

Negro and *Caucasian* are always capitalized, but *blacks, whites,* or slang words for the races are lowercased.

---

54. Capitalize scientific names for genus, but not species.

Drosophila melanogaster (abbreviated *D. melanogaster*)
Homo sapiens

NOTE: Do not capitalize the seasons.
Do not capitalize a.m. or p.m.

NUMBERS–Figures or Words?

A few conventions regarding the writing of numbers should be observed.

55. Spell out numbers in the following cases:

a) at the beginning of a sentence

Fifteen men on the Dead Man's Chest. – Robert Louis Stevenson

b) when the number is less than 10 and does not appear in the same sentence with larger numbers *

Sometimes I've believed as many as six impossible things before breakfast. – Lewis Carroll

c) to represent round numbers of indefinite expressions

several thousand people
the roaring Twenties
between two and three hundred employees
in her eighties

d) fractions standing alone or followed by *of a* or *of an*

one-fourth inch two-thirds of a cup
two one-hundredths one-half of an apple

e) preceding a unit modifier that contains a figure

three 8-foot planks six 1/2-inch strips

---

* I use here the convention adopted by the Canadian Press *Style Book.* Some texts state that numbers less than 100 should be written as words, but current usage favors 10 as the dividing point.

56. Use figures to represent numbers in the following cases:

a) when the number itself is 10 or more

b) when numbers below 10 occur with larger numbers and refer to the same general subject

> I have ordered 9 cups of coffee, 6 cups of tea, and 15 sandwiches to be delivered in one hour.

> (The number *one* in "one hour" is not related to the other numbers and thus is not written as a figure.)

c) when they refer to parts of a book

Chapter 9	page 75
Table I	Figure 5

d) when they precede units of time, measurement, or money

18 years old	2 x 4 centimetres
9 o'clock or 9.00	3 hours 30 minutes 12 seconds
$1.50	75¢
1/4-millimetre pipe	10 litres

NOTE: Units of time, measurement, and money do not affect the rule determining use of figures when numbers appear elsewhere in a sentence (see Rule 56b, above). For example:

Wrong: The 3 students collected $50 apiece.

Right: The three students collected $50 apiece.

SPELLING

There is no better cure for bad spelling than lots of good reading, with a mind alert to the appearance of the words. Frequent dictionary use is also essential. However, a few rules may prove useful.

57. Forming plurals:

   a) if the noun ends in *o*

when preceded by a vowel, **always** add *s*

studios	cameos
kangaroos	patios
rodeos	zoos

when preceded by a consonant, **usually** add *es*

potatoes	innuendoes
heroes	torpedoes

but, musical terms ending in *o* add only *s*

solos	pianos
banjos	sextos

and there are other words ending in *o* where you add only *s*

radios	mementos
zeros	avocados

plus about 40 more. If in doubt, consult your dictionary.

   b) nouns ending in *s, x, ch, sh,* and *z,* add *es*

boxes	beaches
bushes	bosses

c) nouns ending in *y*

when preceded by a consonant, change the *y* to *i* and add *es*

company	companies
authority	authorities
category	categories
parody	parodies

when preceded by a vowel, simply add *s*

attorney	attorneys
money	moneys*

*Moneys is the preferred plural, according to most modern dictionaries, but it is occasionally spelled *monies.*

d) compound words

Form plurals with the principal word.

notaries public	mothers-in-law
attorneys general	major generals
deputy chiefs of staff	commanders in chief

If the words are of equal weight, make both plural.

coats of arms	men employees
secretaries-treasurers	women writers

Nouns ending with *-ful*, add *s* to the end of the word,

cupfuls	teaspoonfuls

unless you wish to convey the use of more than one container. In that case, write as two words and make the noun plural.

cups full (separate cups)
buckets full (separate buckets)

NOTE: Form possessives of **singular** compound words at the end of the last word (*mother-in-law's, attorney general's*). Indicate possessives of **plural** compound words without the use of an apostrophe (the meeting of the attorneys general, *not* the attorneys general's meeting).

---

e) acronyms, numbers, and letters

As much as possible without creating confusion, simply add *s* to plurals.

VIPs	the three Rs
in twos and threes	the late 1960s

But abbreviations with a period or lowercase letters require an apostrophe as well.

I.O.U.'s·	x's and y's

f) foreign words

Certain words (primarily Latin in origin) form plurals according to their foreign derivation. Some of the most common are listed below, followed by examples of foreign words whose plural forms have become Anglicized. A recent edition of a good dictionary is your best guide.

Singular	Plural
alumnus (masc.)	alumni (masc. *or* masc. and fem.)
alumna (fem.)	alumnae (fem.)
axis	axes
crisis	crises
criterion	criteria
datum	data
medium	media
memorandum	memoranda *or* memorandums
nucleus	nuclei
phenomenon	phenomena
stimulus	stimuli
stratum	strata

Note the singular form of *criteria* and *phenomena*. A common mistake is the use of the plural form instead of *criterion* or *phenomenon*. The word *data* is also frequently misused. Although it is popularly treated as singular, in formal writing (especially scientific) you should treat it as the plural word it is. Thus, data *are*, not data *is*.

Anglicized Plurals

antenna	antennas
appendix	appendixes
cactus	cactuses
formula	formulas
index	indexes (scientific, use *indices*)
prospectus	prospectuses

58. Adding Suffixes:

Double the final consonant when all of the following conditions are met:

suffix begins with a vowel
(-*e*d, -*a*ble, -*i*ng)

word ends in a single consonant that is preceded by a single vowel
(swi*m*, gri*n*, fla*p*)

last syllable is accented, or the word consists of one syllable
(remit, rip, put)

The following words do *not* meet at least one of the above requirements, and thus the final consonant is not doubled:

commit   commitment
(suffix does not begin with a vowel)

appeal   appealed
(final consonant is preceded by a double vowel)

render   rendered
(last syllable is not accented)

39

The following words *do* meet the requirements:

bag	baggage
red	reddish
occur	occurrence
refer	referred
transfer	transferred
commit	committed

NOTE: If the accent moves to the preceding syllable with the addition of a suffix, the final consonant is not doubled.

refer	reference
prefer	preference

---

59. Words ending in *-able* or *-ible*

We have no convenient, watertight rule for determining whether to add *-able* or *-ible*. But here's a slightly helpful guide:

Any word that has an *-ation* form **always** takes the suffix *-able*.

> durable (duration)
> commendable (commendation)
> irritable (irritation)
> excitable (excitation)

Words with *-ion, -tion, -id,* or *-ive* forms **usually** take the suffix *-ible*.

> collectible (collection)
> irresistible (resistive)
> digestible (digestion)
> suggestible (suggestive)

But remember this is not completely reliable. For example, some words that do not have an *-ation* form nonetheless take *-able* (manageable, desirable, likable). A dictionary will solve the problem if you are uncertain.

40

60. Words ending in *-sede, -ceed,* **and** *-cede.*

Only one word ends in *-sede* (supersede), and three end in *-ceed* (exceed, proceed, succeed). All other words of this type end in *-cede* (precede, secede...).

> *Nothing succeeds like excess.* – Oscar Wilde

61. *ei* **and** *ie* **words**

The grammar school jingle we all learned has so many exceptions that you should use it only when you don't have a dictionary handy. The first line of the jingle is the more useful part.

> Put *i* before *e*, except after *c*,

(*i* before *e*): piece, brief, niece
(except after *c*): receive, ceiling, deceive

This rule applies only when the words containing *ei* or *ie* are pronounced like *ee* (as in *need*). When the sound is other than *ee*, the correct spelling is usually *ei* (e.g., freight, vein). Some exceptions are *either/neither, seize, financier,* and *weird.*

WORD DIVISION

Words that are divided at the right-hand margin are an interruption to the reader; incorrectly divided words slow the reader down even more. So divide words only when you must, and always do it correctly. Both parts of a divided word should be pronounceable, and you should avoid breaking a word so that the first fragment produces a misleading meaning (legis-lature, not leg-islature; peas-ant, not pea-sant).

62. **Divide words as follows:**

   a) between syllables

num-ber	moun-tain
con-sonant	egg-head
know-ledge	prod-uct

   Careful pronunciation will help you determine correct syllabication.

   b) between double letters

quar-rel	refer-ring
com-mittee	accom-modate

   unless the double letter comes at the end of the simple form of the word

call-ing	bless-ing
success-ful	add-ing

   c) in hyphenated words, only where the hyphen already exists

   thirty-five, not thir-ty-five

   d) at a prefix or suffix, but not within it

   super-market, not su-permarket
   contra-ceptive, not con-traceptive

42

e) to produce the most meaningful grouping

careless-ness, not care-lessness
consign-ment, not con-signment

f) after a one-letter syllable

busi-ness   deli-cate

unless the one-letter syllable is part of the suffixes *-able* or *-ible*

illeg-ible   mov-able
inevit-able   permiss-ible

NOTE: The *a* and *i* in many *-able* and *-ible* words are not one-letter syllables and should be divided as in the following examples:

    ame-na-ble   pos-si-ble
    ter-ri-ble   char-i-ta-ble
    ca-pa-ble   swim-ma-ble

---

63. **Do not divide the following:**

a) one-syllable words

b) words with fewer than six letters

c) one-letter syllables

alone, not a-lone   eu-phoria, not euphori-a

d) two-letter syllables at the end of a word

caller, not call-er   pur-chaser, not purchas-er
walked, not walk-ed   leader, not lead-er

Another way of stating the last two rules (c & d) is that you should leave at least two letters before the hyphen and three letters after it.

e) these suffixes

-cial	-cion	-cious	-tious
-tial	-sion	-ceous	-geous
-sial	-tion	-gion	-gious

f) abbreviations, contractions, or a person's name

g) the last word of a paragraph or last word on a page

64. **When three or more consonants come together, let pronunciation be your guide.**

punc-ture	match-ing
chil-dren	birth-day

When in doubt, consult a dictionary, where you will find the words divided into syllables.

Grammatical Guidelines

GRAMMATICAL GUIDELINES

One of the best ways to get a grip on grammar is to develop an ear for the sound of properly used language. Ironically, at a time when our ears are bombarded by radio and television, your best bet for exposure to the "sound" of correct grammar still lies in the visual act of reading good prose.

> *It is only in good writing that you will find how words are best used, what shades of meaning they can be made to carry, and by what devices (or lack of them) the reader is kept going smoothly or bogged down.* — Jacques Barzun

Listen to the words and develop a sympathy for the reader who is trying to make sense of them.

65. Subject and verb must agree both in person and number.

This rule seems to top everyone's list. Jacques Barzun has some good words on the subject:

> *Agreement is as pleasant in prose as it is in personal relations, and no more difficult to work for.*

Theodore Bernstein devotes five pages to the subject in his book, *The Careful Writer*. He claims errors in agreement are the most common mistakes writers make.

On the surface, the rule seems simple: A verb must agree with its subject both in person and number. Thus, a singular subject requires a singular verb. *(Tom is late.)* A plural or compound subject requires a plural verb. *(Tom and Bill are late.)* A subject in the first person requires a verb in the first person. *(I am exasperated.)* A subject in the third person requires a verb in the third person. *(She is exasperated.)* And so on.

Applying this rule can be difficult. For example, it is not always clear which word or phrase is the subject. And even if the subject is easy to identify, it may not be clear whether it is singular or plural. The most common trouble spots regarding agreement of subject and verb are presented below in those two general categories: identifying the subject and determining the number.

a) Identifying the Subject

(1) Intervening Phrases

Phrases that come between subject and verb do not affect the number of the verb.

> The *purpose* of his speeches *was* to win votes.

> The company's total *salaries*, exclusive of overtime, *are* $2000 per week.

> *One* of the reasons he was late for dinner *was* that his watch had stopped.

The subjects of the above sentences are *purpose, salaries,* and *one,* respectively. By mentally leaving out the phrases that come between those subjects and their verbs, you can determine if a singular or plural verb is required.

(2) Phrases and Clauses as Subject

When the subject of a sentence is a phrase or clause, it takes a singular verb. The subjects of the following sentences are *Waiting for someone to arrive* and *What this country needs*.

> Waiting for someone to arrive makes time drag.

> *What this country needs is a good 5¢ nickel.* — F. P. Adams

(3) Inverted Sentence Order

The subject usually precedes the verb. But when the subject follows the verb, it is sometimes hard to tell if the verb should be singular or plural. In the following example, the subject is *Margaret Atwood,* not *popular authors*, and a singular verb is correct.

Leading the list of popular authors was Margaret Atwood.

In the following sentence the compound subject *a group of taxpayers and their M.L.A.* requires a plural verb.

Seeking to defeat the amendment were a group of taxpayers and their M.L.A.

First locate the subject and then you will know what the number of the verb should be.

b) Determining the Number

(1) Compound Subjects

Two subjects joined by *and* are a compound subject, and they require a plural verb.

The title and abstract of the report are printed on the first page.

Writing a report and filing it are difficult tasks for the new manager.

NOTE: The following are exceptions to the preceding rule:

If the two parts of the compound subject are regarded as one unit, they take a singular verb.

Bacon and eggs is a good way to start the day.

Compound subjects preceded by *each* or *every* are singular.

Every man, woman, and child is given full consideration.

Each nut and bolt is individually wrapped.

Company names, though they may combine several units or names, are considered as a single entity and thus take a singular verb.

Jones and Associates is a management consulting firm.

Best, Best, & Best Co. is a major department store.

(2) Collective Nouns

Nouns such as *family, couple, group, people, majority, percent,* or *personnel* take either singular or plural verbs. If the word refers to the group as a whole or the idea of oneness predominates, use a singular verb.

The group is meeting tonight at seven.

The elderly couple was the last to arrive.

A minority may be right; a majority is always wrong. —Henrik Ibsen

But if the word refers to individuals within a group, use a plural verb.

A group of 19th century paintings and statues were donated to the museum.

A couple of latecomers were escorted to their seats.

50

Similarly, words ending in *-ics* (e.g., *statistics, athletics, politics, economics*) take either singular or plural verbs, depending on their use.

Statistics is a difficult subject. (singular)

The statistics show a decreasing birth rate. (plural)

Politics offers yesterday's answers to today's problems.
— Marshall McLuhan

The word *number* is singular when preceded by *the* and plural when preceded by *a*.

A number of stock market indicators *were* favorable.

The number of students enrolling in college *is* decreasing.

(3) Indefinite Pronouns

The following pronouns are always singular: *another, each, every, either, neither,* and *one*, as are the compound pronouns made with *any, every, some,* and *no: anybody, anything, anyone, nobody, nothing, no one*, etc.

Neither of the tax returns *was* completed correctly.

Each of you *is* welcome.

Every dog has his day. — Cervantes

Nothing is so useless as a general maxim. — Macaulay

NOTE: When the word *each* **follows** a plural subject, it does not affect the verb, which remains plural.

The voters each have their own opinion.

The following pronouns are always plural: *both, few, many, others,* and *several.*

> *Many are called, but few are chosen.* — Matthew 22:14

The following pronouns are either singular or plural, depending on the noun referred to: *all, none, any, some, more,* and *most.*

All the milk is gone. (singular)
All the mistakes were avoidable. (plural)
None of the laundry was properly cleaned. (singular)
Three people were in the plane, but none was hurt. (singular)
None are more lonesome than long-distance runners. (plural)

It may help to note that when *none* means "no one" or "not one," it takes a singular verb; when it means "not any" or "no amount," it takes a plural verb.

(4) Either/or, Neither/nor Constructions

The verb is singular when the elements that are connected by *either/or* or *neither/nor* are singular:

Neither his teacher nor his mother was able to help.

> *Neither snow, nor rain, nor heat, nor gloom of night stays these couriers from their appointed rounds.* — Herodotus

If the elements that are combined are plural, the verb is plural:

Either personal cheques or major credit cards are satisfactory methods of payment.

If the elements combined are both singular and plural, the number of the element immediately preceding the verb determines the number of the verb:

Neither the twins nor their cousin is coming to the party.

> *Either war is obsolete or men are.* — Buckminster Fuller

52

(5) Expressions of Time, Money, and Quantity

If a total amount is indicated, use a singular verb:

Ten dollars is a reasonable price.

If the reference is to individual units, use a plural verb:

Ten dollar bills are enclosed.

(6) Fractions

The number of the noun following a fraction determines the number of the verb:

Three-fourths of the ballots have been counted. (plural)

Three-fourths of the money is missing. (singular)

Democracy is the recurrent suspicion that more than half of the people are right more than half of the time. — E. B. White

---

NOTE: Agreement between *pronoun* and subject is as important as between *verb* and subject.

Each student is bringing his (not *their*) own books.

The Progressive Conservative party has nominated its (not *their*) candidate.

The employees are bringing their (not *his* or *her*) own bag lunches.

Some people use the word *their* to overcome sexist implications of using *his* or the awkwardness of *his or her*. While not strictly correct, this usage may come to be accepted in this day of liberated pronouns.

---

66. Use parallel construction.

Parallel thoughts should be expressed in grammatically parallel terms. Thus, you can have a sequence of gerunds or infinitives, but not a gerund followed by an infinitive:

Wrong: Swimming is better exercise than to ski.

Right: Swimming is better exercise than skiing.

Wrong: The students came on foot, by car, and bicycle.

Right: The students came on foot, by car, and by bicycle.

Wrong: in spring, in summer, and fall

Right: in spring, in summer, and in fall

This principle is also important in numbered lists, outlines, or headings.

1. Select the team.

2. Train the team.

3. Evaluate the team (*not* Evaluating the team).

Use parallel words, phrases, clauses, verbs, and tenses to improve the flow of ideas and heighten impact. Similarity of form helps the reader recognize similarity of content or function.

We think according to nature; we speak according to rules; we act according to custom. — Francis Bacon

Canada has no cultural unity, no linguistic unity, no religious unity, no economic unity, no geographic unity. All it has is unity.
— Kenneth Boulding

67. Avoid misplaced modifiers.

Keep related words together and in the order that conveys the intended meaning.

> We almost lost all of the crop.

> We lost almost all of the crop.

Both are correct grammatically, but only one accurately describes the situation. To avoid this type of confusion, place adverbs directly *preceding* the word or phrase they modify.

The following examples indicate the kind of predicament you can create if you misplace a modifier.

> We saw a man on a horse with a wooden leg.

> The sunbather watched the soaring seagulls wearing a striped bikini.

> The politician met informally to discuss food prices and the high cost of living with several women.

> The fire was extinguished before any damage was done by the Fire Department.

> Be sure to purchase enough yarn to finish the sweater before you start.

> He told her that he wanted to marry her frequently.

68. Avoid dangling modifiers.

A dangling modifier gives the false impression that it modifies a word or group of words, but what it modifies has actually been left out of the sentence. For example:

Wrong: After writing the introduction, the rest of the report was easy.

After writing the introduction appears to modify *the rest of the report*. But obviously *the rest of the report* did not do the writing. Whoever did the writing has been omitted. Correct versions would be:

Right: After I wrote the introduction, the rest of the report was easy.

After writing the introduction, he found the rest of the report easy.

Other examples of dangling modifiers:

Weighing the alternatives carefully, a decision was reached.

At the age of five, his father died.

When dipped in butter, you can taste the lobster's delicious flavor.

These should be rewritten as follows:

Weighing the alternatives carefully, we reached a decision.

At the age of five, the boy became an orphan.

When dipped in butter, the lobster tastes delicious.

Dangling modifiers frequently result in ridiculous statements:

Being old and dog-eared, I was able to buy the book for 50¢.

Walking along the shore, a fish suddenly jumped out of the water.

Certain modifying phrases, though they may seem only loosely related to the words that follow, are acceptable. Examples are *all things considered*, *strictly speaking*, and *judging by the record*.

Some Specifics of Style

SOME SPECIFICS OF STYLE

69. Omit unnecessary words.
If I were limited to one rule of style, Omit Unnecessary Words would be the hands-down winner. Variously described as *fog* or even *windy-foggery*, excess words creep into our writing from a number of directions.

Perhaps the most obvious source of wordiness is the governmentalese kind of jargon that has evolved and flourished until it threatens to drown us in paper. The basic premise of this type of writing is that the impressiveness of a document is in direct proportion to the length of its words and the convolutedness of its sentences. Typical results of this attitude are the following real-life examples:

> "Our proposal follows the sequential itemization of points occurring elsewhere in your RFP, wherever possible, to facilitate your review..."

Translation: We will follow your outline.

> "Evaluation and Parameterization of Stability and Safety Performance Characteristics of Two and Three Wheeled Vehicular Toys for Riding"

Translation: Why Children Fall Off Bicycles*

Another source of wordiness is the redundancy and sloppy usage we have built into the language over the years. "General consensus of opinion" uses four words where only one is correct; "consensus" *means* collective opinion, general agreement and accord. "Hot water heater": It's really a cold water heater, right? "Water heater" would suffice.

---

*The first of these monstrosities is a direct quote from a document I edited, and the second was cited in a military publication.

The following phrases are typical of our tendency to use several words where one would do:

eliminate completely	future plans
chief protagonist	advance warning
temporary reprieve	spell out in detail
may possibly	completely unanimous
small in size	various different
absolutely essential	complete monopoly

"Whether or not" is frequently best stated as simply "whether." All phrases built around "the fact that," "there is," and "there are" probably could be cut with no loss.

The economy may be inflated, but our writing need not be. Avoid such overblown expressions as the following:

it is often the case that = frequently
in the event that = if
be of the opinion that = believe
be in possession of = have
owing to the fact that = since or because
the fact that he had arrived = his arrival
on the order of = about
in advance of = before
in spite of the fact that = although
is indicative of = indicates
had occasion to be = was
put in an appearance = appeared
take into consideration = consider

Look with a fresh eye upon these verbal barnacles, and keep scraping them off.

In the rush to put our ideas on paper, we frequently use words that are not only unnecessary but actually obscure what we are trying to convey. As with other sources of wordiness, the best cure is to revise, revise, and revise again. Edit once looking strictly for spare words. When you think you have pruned every one, review the document once more to see if you missed any.

A sampling of comments on this theme follows:

> *In composing, as a general rule, run your pen through every other word you have written; you have no idea what vigor it will give to your style.* — Sydney Smith

> *Vigorous writing is concise. A sentence should contain no unnecessary words, a paragraph no unnecessary sentences, for the same reason that a drawing should have no unnecessary lines and a machine no unnecessary parts. This requires not that the writer make all his sentences short, or that he avoid all detail and treat his subjects only in outline, but that every word tell.* — William Strunk, Jr.

> *It is often harder to boil down than to write.*
> — Sir William Osler

> *Communication is most complete when it proceeds from the smallest number of words—and indeed of syllables.*
> — Jacques Barzun

70. Use active voice and positive form.
The difference between active and passive voice is the difference between *The manager received the letter* and *The letter was received by the manager.*

Passive voice almost always violates the Omit Unnecessary Words Rule (five words vs. seven in the example above). Furthermore, it lacks the vigor and forcefulness of the active voice.

> A trend is shown by the study...(passive)
>
> The study shows a trend...(active)
>
> The man was bitten by the dog...(passive)
>
> The dog bit the man...(active)

The positive form also has more vigor and force than negative.

> They did not often arrive on time. (negative)
>
> They usually arrived late. (positive)

Watch for the word *not* and see if you can restate the idea more effectively.

Hamlet's chief flaw was that he was not very decisive.

Hamlet's chief flaw was his indecisiveness.

Replace:	with:
did not remember	forgot
was not present	was absent
did not pay attention to	ignored

Sometimes the negative form is appropriate for the desired effect. Reserve its use for those instances.

She is not unattractive.

Not that I loved Caesar less, but that I loved Rome more.
— Shakespeare

He knows not his own strength that hath not met adversity.
— Francis Bacon

71. Be specific and concrete.

Avoid vagueness. A "scientist" may be more accurately identified as a physicist, chemist, or electrical engineer. "The present writer" is a coy way of avoiding the use of "I."

Wherever possible, replace abstract words with concrete ones:

Abstract:	Concrete:
vehicle	bicycle
food	steak
color	red
emotion	hatred

In the following quotation, George Orwell has drained the juices from a Biblical passage and translated it into the vague and all-too-familiar prose that we find in business and scientific circles:

Objective consideration of contemporary phenomena compels the conclusion that success or failure in competitive activities exhibits no tendency to be commensurate with innate capacity, but that a considerable element of the unpredictable must inevitably be taken into account.

Notice the contrast in word length and concreteness when compared with the original verse from Ecclesiastes:

I returned, and saw under the sun, that the race is not to the wise, nor yet riches to men of understanding, nor yet favor to men of skill; but time and chance happeneth to them all.

Which leads us to a related rule:

72. Use simple words.
Avoid the four- or five-syllable word when one or two syllables convey the idea just as well.

Replace:	with:
utilize	use
ameliorate	improve
modification	change
deficiency	lack
preventative	preventive

73. Avoid overworked words or phrases.
Television and newspapers can turn a popular phrase into a raging epidemic overnight. The best way to stifle these verbal plagues is to shun the "in" word or phrase until it has had time to cool off and can be restored to its appropriate, occasional use. *The bottom line, at this point in time, bite the bullet,* and *male chauvinist pig,* for example, suggest a shortage of original thought.

As H. W. Fowler points out in *A Dictionary of Modern English*, hackneyed phrases should be danger signals that the author is writing "bad stuff, or it would not need such help. Let him see to the substance of his cake instead of decorating it with sugarplums."

Fads can be profitable for manufacturers of hula hoops or hot tubs, but word fads profit no one.

74. Eliminate jargon.
The word *jargon* derives from Middle English, "meaningless chatter," which in turn comes from Old French, "twittering." These roots clearly indicate why jargon should be avoided. The following are examples of different types of jargon.

a) Bastard Words
A noun plus a suffix such as *-ize* or *-wise* creates commercial jargon. *Finalize, prioritize, budgetwise*, and *taxwise* are examples. Wherever possible, rewrite to avoid these coined words.

b) Nouns and Adjectives Converted into Verbs
If making a noun or adjective into a verb avoids an awkward or wordy construction, it is justifiable.

> The motion was tabled.

But find other ways of saying:

> The information was inputted.

> This model obsoletes all its predecessors.

> The book was authored by...

c) Noun-Noun Constructions

Government and business documents abound with jammed-together constructions such as:

community work experience program demonstration project

Break up these chains of nouns into more understandable arrangements. For example, the above six-noun chain could be written:

a program to show the value of community work

Although you may use a few more words when you break up a noun chain, the result is a more understandable phrase. Eliminating words *can* be carried too far.

75. Vary sentence length and construction.

Retain reader interest by varying sentence length and by using clauses and phrases in different constructions. A series of short declarative sentences is fine for instructions, but once past the Dick-and-Jane stage, most readers appreciate variety. As you re-read what you have written, notice its rhythm—is it choppy, sing-song, lively, flowing? Make the rhythm of the sentences appropriate for your purpose.

76. Watch out for the word *very*.

The word *very* often signals sloppy writing. Overusing it weakens rather than intensifies your meaning.

Poor: His response was very quick and very emphatic.
Better: His response was quick and emphatic.

In some cases, using *very* is simply incorrect:

Wrong: His approach was very unique.
          Her words were very final.

Words such as *unique* and *final* stand by themselves; do not attempt to make them more emphatic by adding the word *very*.

If you feel *very* is needed to strengthen a word, you should
consider whether another word that doesn't require such
buttressing would be more effective:

very stubborn	obstinate, bullheaded
very weak	frail, feeble, fragile
very surprised	astonished, astounded, amazed

Postscript concerning Sexism in Language

The topic of sexist language has provoked considerable debate
in recent years. Some people feel such concern is misplaced and
wonder why we should worry about the masculine bias of
language. There are two pragmatic reasons for being
concerned: reducing confusion and avoiding possible offence.
If we use the masculine pronoun *he* to refer to both sexes, the
reader may wonder if, in fact, both sexes are included. If we
address a letter to an unknown person as *Dear Sir* or
Gentlemen, we may prejudice the reader against us. Revising to
eliminate bias is indeed a valid objective.

Progress has been made in some areas. For example, I find *Ms.*
to be helpful in the old *Miss/Mrs.* dilemma. I'm even inclined to
agree that a woman's marital status should not be incorporated
into the form of address we use, just as it is not indicated by the
word *Mr.* Changing such terms as *workmen's compensation* to
worker's compensation is easily done and worthwhile.

However, the goal of a sex-neutral language has been carried
beyond reason by those who advocate using a substitute for the
syllable *man* wherever it occurs. Words such as *manipulate* or
manufacture are derived from the Latin *manus* (hand); they
have no roots in common with our word *man* and present no
problem of ambiguity.

Nonsexist writing is better writing. Finding ways to avoid sexist
terms is largely a matter of motivation. Some suggestions can
be found in my book entitled *Better Letters: A Handbook of
Business & Personal Correspondence* and in a fine book by
Casey Miller and Kate Swift, *The Handbook of Nonsexist
Writing* (see Bibliography).

Confused and Abused Words

advice/advise
affect/effect
allude/refer
allusion/illusion
alright
alternate/alternative
ante/anti
bi/semi
can/may
capital/capitol
complement/compliment
continual/continuous
council/counsel/consul
different from/different than
discreet/discrete
disinterested/uninterested
economic/economical
eminent/imminent
enthuse
etc.
farther/further
fewer/less

firstly/secondly
flammable/inflammable
foreword/forward
fortuitous/fortunate
hopefully
I/me/myself
imply/infer
insure/ensure/assure
irregardless
it's/its
lay/lie
lend/loan
like/as
loose/lose
meantime/meanwhile
people/persons
principal/principle
shall/will
stationary/stationery
that/which
was/were
which/who
who/whom

CONFUSED AND ABUSED WORDS

The difference between the right word and the almost right word is the difference between lightning and the lightning bug. — Mark Twain

The following list may help you tell the difference.

Advice/Advise: The noun *advice* means suggestion or counsel; the verb *advise* means to give advice.

I advise you not to take her advice.

Affect/Effect: Perhaps the easiest way to sort out the confusion about these two words is to remember that the most common use of *affect* is as a verb, and of *effect* is as a noun.

The verb *affect* means to influence or to produce an effect on.

The lawyer hoped to affect the jury's decision.

A less common meaning of *affect* as a verb is to pretend, to simulate, or imitate in order to make some desired impression.

The lawyer affected a look of disbelief when the defendant was unable to recall his whereabouts.

The noun *effect* means result or consequence.

The lawyer's closing statement had an effect on the jury.

The verb *effect* means to bring about.

The new manager effected many changes in personnel.

Chances are that if the sentence calls for a verb, *affect* is the word you want; if the sentence calls for a noun, *effect* is the appropriate word.

69

Allude/Refer: To *allude* to something is to mention it indirectly, without identifying it specifically. To *refer* is to indicate directly.

The speaker alluded to the hazards of obesity when he referred to the chart showing life expectancy and weight.

Allusion/Illusion: *Allusion*, the noun form of the verb *allude*, means an indirect reference to something not specifically identified, while *illusion* is a mistaken perception.

Alright: Common misspelling of the words *all right*.

Alternate/Alternative: *Alternate* refers to every other one, or following by turns; *alternative* is a choice.

Ante/Anti: *Ante-* means before or in front of. *Anti-* means against.

The people in the anteroom are all anti-nuclear protesters.

Bi/Semi: You won't find 100 percent agreement among experts, but most favor the use of *bi-*, as in *bimonthly* or *biweekly*, to mean every two months or weeks. The prefix *semi-* is reserved for the meaning of half or occurring twice within the time period. Thus, a bimonthly meeting would take place every two months, and a semimonthly meeting would occur twice each month. An exception is biannual, which means twice a year; biennial means every two years.

Can/May: Written usage requires that you distinguish between *can* and *may*; *can* means ability or power to do something, *may* means permission to do it.

You may have dessert if you can eat your vegetables.

Capital/Capitol: *Capital* refers to wealth, the city that is the seat of government, or an upper case letter. *Capitol* is the building in which government officials congregate, and it is used most frequently in the U.S. The *Capitol*, when referring to the home of the U.S. Congress, is always capitalized.

The Prime Minister will visit U.S. senators at the Capitol.

Complement/Compliment: *Complement* is both a verb and a noun, meaning to complete a whole or satisfy a need. *Compliment* means praise and also functions as both verb and noun.

His efforts complemented those of the rest of the team. (verb)

A complement of 12 soldiers performed the assignment. (noun)

She complimented him on the apple pie he had baked. (verb)

Her compliment was sincere. (noun)

Nowadays we are all of us so hard up that the only pleasant things to pay are compliments. — Oscar Wilde

Continual/Continuous: *Continual* means over and over again, whereas *continuous* should only be used to mean uninterrupted or unbroken.

Since he coughed continually, the doctor kept him under continuous observation.

A man's memory may almost become the art of continually varying and misrepresenting his past, according to his interests in the present. — George Santayana

Council/Counsel/Consul: *Council*, always a noun, refers to an assemblage of persons or a committee. *Counsel* has both verb and noun forms, meaning to advise, the advice itself, or an attorney.

Counsel for the defense counselled the defense not to speak to the council members; the council resented his counsel.

Consul is a person in the foreign service of a country.

Different from/Different than: *Different from* is preferred when it is followed by a noun or short phrase.

His writing style is different from mine.

Different than is acceptable when its use avoids wordiness or when *different* is followed by a clause.

Today the concept of women's rights is different than it was at the turn of the century.

Discreet/Discrete: *Discreet* is used to describe behavior that is prudent or respectful of propriety. *Discrete* frequently has a scientific connotation and means separate, distinct, or individual.

He made discreet inquiries into her whereabouts.

The smooth surface of water seems to contradict the discrete nature of its molecules.

Disinterested/Uninterested: *Disinterested* should only be used to convey objectivity or neutrality, while *uninterested* is simply lacking interest.

A disinterested scientist would not necessarily be uninterested in the results of the experiment.

Economic/Economical: *Economic* means of or pertaining to the production, development, and management of material wealth. *Economical* means not wasteful.

The economic impact of the Depression forced most families to adopt economical measures.

Eminent/Imminent: *Eminent* means well known or distinguished, while *imminent* means about to happen.

The arrival of the eminent statesman was imminent.

Enthuse: An informal form of the word *enthusiastic* that is not acceptable in formal writing. Rewrite to avoid its use.

Etc.: From Latin *et cetera* meaning "and others." *Etc.* is inappropriate in formal writing. In general, you should rewrite to avoid its use. Never write **and** *etc.*

Lost & Found Departments are usually filled with items such as umbrellas, hats, and single gloves. (*not* umbrellas, hats, single gloves, etc.)

Farther/Further: *Farther* should be reserved for ideas of physical distance. Use *further* in all other senses, specifically when indicating additional time, degree, or quantity.

We walked farther than we had intended.

The jury expressed the need for further deliberation.

The distinction between these two words will probably disappear eventually; as Theodore Bernstein points out in *The Careful Writer*, "It looks as if *farther* is going to be mowed down by the scythe of Old Further Time."

Fewer/Less: Generally, *less* is used for quantity, *fewer* for number.

Fewer potatoes, less mush.

Fewer is preferred when referring to individual numbers or units, while *less* is used in sentences involving periods of time, sums of money, or measures of distance and weight.

Automation requires more machines and fewer people.

He ran the mile in less than four minutes.

Firstly/Secondly: Just using *first* and *second* is sufficient and avoids the whole controversy over whether the *-ly* form of the word is correct.

Flammable/Inflammable: Both mean capable of burning.

Foreword/Forward: *Foreword* is a preface or introductory note. Notice the spelling: It deals with words and is spelled with an *o*. *Forward* means the opposite of backward. There is no such word as *foreward*.

Fortuitous/Fortunate: *Fortuitous* means by chance or accidental. *Fortunate* means lucky.

73

Hopefully: Means with hope, in a hopeful manner. Frequently — and incorrectly — used with the meaning of "it is to be hoped" or "I hope."

I/Me/Myself: *I* is the subjective case and thus should be used when it is the subject of the sentence (the *who* or *what* that the rest of the sentence is about):

> My brother and I went to the ballgame.

Me is the objective case and should be used when it is the object of the action or thought conveyed by the verb of the sentence, or is the object of a preposition:

> Between you and me, I hate Sunday afternoon football games.

> Stan invited Mark and me to a beach party.

In a sentence like the last, if you remove "Mark and," it quickly becomes obvious that *me* is the correct pronoun.

Myself is used for emphasis:

> I'd rather do it myself.

or as a reflexive pronoun (i.e., turning the action back on the grammatical subject):

> I was able to feed myself when I was very young.

It is incorrect to use *myself* as a substitute for *I* or *me*.

Wrong: The gift was presented to both my brother and myself.

Right: The gift was presented to both my brother and me.

Wrong: My partner and myself have entered into a new agreement.

Right: My partner and I have entered into a new agreement.

Imply/Infer: To *imply* is to suggest indirectly or insinuate; to *infer* is to draw a conclusion or deduce. Generally, a speaker implies and listeners infer.

Insure/Ensure/Assure: All three words mean to make secure or certain.

Victory is assured (or ensured or insured).

Assure has the meaning of setting someone's mind at rest. Both *ensure* and *insure* mean to make secure from harm. Only *insure* should be used regarding guaranteeing of life or property against risk.

Irregardless: A redundancy. Use *regardless*.

It's/Its: *It's* is the contraction of *it is*. *Its* is a possessive pronoun.

Lay/Lie: *Lay* is a transitive verb (i.e., it takes an object) meaning to place or put down.

Lay the package on the table. (*Package* is the object of the verb *lay*.)

Lie is an intransitive verb (i.e., it does not take an object) meaning to recline.

Lie on your exercise mat.

Lend/Loan: *Lend* is a verb, and *loan* is primarily a noun. However, the use of *loan* as a verb seems to be more and more prevalent, and it completely dominates business circles. If the past tense of *lend* sounds awkward, use *loan*.

She loaned the museum three paintings.

The bank loaned the company $100,000.

But wherever possible, hold the line on abuses of the word. For instance, say "Lend me your pen," not "Loan me your pen."

Like/As: *Like* is correct when it functions as a preposition.

She sang like an angel.

My Luv is like a red, red rose. — Robert Burns

Like is also acceptable when it introduces a clause in which the verb has been omitted.

> She took to politics like a fish to water.

As should be used instead of *like* when the clause includes a verb.

> She took to politics as a fish takes to water.

Like as a conjunction is generally unacceptable and should be replaced by *as, as if,* or *as though.*

> Truffles taste good, as an epicurean dish should.

> *We can act as if there were a God; feel as if we were free; consider Nature as if she were full of special designs; lay plans as if we were to be immortal; and we find then that these words do make a genuine difference in our moral life.* — William James

Loose/Lose: *Loose* is an adjective meaning unrestrained or not fastened. *Lose* is a verb meaning the opposite of win or the opposite of find.

Meantime/Meanwhile: *Meantime* is usually a noun describing the interval between one event and other; *meanwhile* is an adverb meaning during or in the intervening time.

> In the meantime, back at the ranch...

> Meanwhile, back at the ranch...

In the meantime and *meanwhile* can usually be interchanged. But do not say *in the meanwhile.*

People/Persons: In general, use *people* for large groups, *persons* for an exact or small number.

> Eight persons are being held as hostages.

> *Hell is—other people!* — Jean Paul Sartre

76

Principal/Principle: *Principal* functions as both noun and adjective. The noun refers to the head of a school or firm, or to capital which earns interest; the adjective means chief or main. *Principle* is a noun meaning rule or standard.

The principal's principal principle was *Do Thy Homework*.

Women without principle draw considerable interest.

Shall/Will: This is one instance where fading of an old grammatical distinction has left us none the poorer. Don't worry about rules regarding *shall* and *will*—just let your ear be your guide. *Shall* is frequently used to express determination.

I shall return. — Douglas MacArthur

Stationary/Stationery: *Stationary* means fixed in one place, not moving. *Stationery* is writing envelopes. A good way to remember is that stationery is what you need to write letters.

That/Which: The *that/which* problem takes up six pages in Fowler's *Dictionary of Modern English Usage*. For most people, it is sufficient to distinguish between the two relative pronouns by using *that* to introduce a restrictive clause (one that is essential to the meaning):

The river that flows by our house is at a low level.

Beware of all enterprises that require new clothes. — Thoreau

and by using *which* to introduce a nonrestrictive or parenthetical clause:

The river, which overflows its banks every year, is now at a low level.

Was/Were: When expressing a wish or a condition contrary to fact, and following the words *as if* and *as though*, use *were*:

The silence made it seem as if he were speaking to an empty room.

If it were not for the presents, an elopement would be preferable.
— George Ade

In expressing a past condition not contrary to fact, use *was*:

> If Deborah was guilty, she did not show it.

Which/Who: Be sure to use *who* when referring to a person and *which* when referring to things.

Who/Whom: The best guide for deciding which of these words to use is to substitute a personal pronoun in place of the word; if *he, she,* or *they* would fit, use *who* (nominative case); if *him, her,* or *them* would fit, use *whom* (objective case).

> This is the man who you thought committed the crime.
> (you thought *he* committed the crime)

> To whom shall I report?
> (to *him, her,* or *them*)

> Champlain, whom we all read about in school . . .
> (we read about *him*)

> Margaret Laurence, who wrote the book . . .
> (*she* wrote)

> *For prying into any human affairs, none are equal to those whom it does not concern.* — Victor Hugo
> (it does not concern *them*)

> *The best liar is he who makes the smallest amount of lying go the longest way.* — Samuel Butler
> (*he* makes the smallest amount)

> *The multitude, who require to be led, still hate their leaders.*
> — William Hazlitt
> (*they* require to be led)

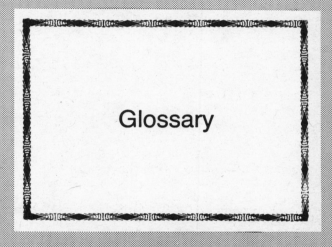

Glossary

GLOSSARY

Active Voice: The form of the verb used when the subject performs the action. See Rule 70, p. 61.

Adjective: Modifies (describes or limits) a noun or pronoun. It may be a single word, phrase, or clause. See Parts of Speech.

> *As to the adjective: when in doubt, strike it out.* — Mark Twain

Adverb: Modifies a verb, an adjective or another adverb. May be a single word, phrase, or clause. See Parts of Speech.

Appositive: A word, phrase, or clause placed near a noun to explain it and having the same grammatical relation to the rest of the sentence as the word it describes.

> My son, *the doctor*, sends me a card every Mother's Day.

Article: The words *a, an,* and *the.*

Case: The means by which the relationship of a noun or pronoun to the rest of the sentence is shown. There are three cases: nominative (also known as subjective), objective, and possessive.

Nominative: the case of the subject of the verb.

> *We* entered the room.

Objective: the case of the object of a verb or preposition.

> He threw the *ball* to *me.*

> (*Ball* is the object of the verb *threw; me* is the object of the preposition *to.*)

Possessive: the case that shows ownership.

> Here is *your* answer.

> Take away the *dog's* bone.

Clause: A group of words that contains a subject and verb.

Co-ordinate clauses have the same rank and are connected by a co-ordinating conjunction.

It started to rain, so we left the football game.

Dependent clauses (also known as subordinate) do not make sense when standing alone.

He watches the late news *before he goes to bed.*

Independent clauses (also called principal or main) are those which would make complete sense if left standing alone.

He watches the late news before going to bed.

Nonrestrictive clauses could be omitted without changing the meaning; they are surrounded by commas.

Sylvia, *who reads a great deal,* has a large vocabulary.

Restrictive clauses are essential to the meaning (i.e., could not be left out without changing the meaning of the sentence).

People *who read a great deal* have large vocabularies.

There are few chaste women who are not tired of their trade.
— LaRochefoucauld

Comma Fault: The error in which a comma is used as the sole connection between two independent clauses.

Wrong: The company picnic is an annual event, this year it will be held at the beach.

The above sentence would be correct if a conjunction such as *and* were added or the comma replaced with a semicolon or period.

82

Complex Sentence: A sentence consisting of one independent clause and one or more dependent (subordinate) clauses. In the following example, the independent clause is underlined; the remaining clauses are dependent.

> <u>A banker is a fellow</u> who lends his umbrella when the sun is shining and wants it back the minute it begins to rain. — Mark Twain

Compound: Consisting of two or more elements.

A *compound adjective*, also known as a unit modifier, consists of two or more adjectives modifying the same noun.

> I'm a tall, gangly, high-bred Canadian who won't be pushed around. — Susan Clark

A *compound sentence* consists of two or more independent clauses.

> Balloonists have an unsurpassed view of the scenery, but there is always the possibility that it may collide with them.
> — H. L. Mencken

A *compound subject* consists of two or more subjects having the same verb.

> Papa, potatoes, poultry, prunes, and prism are all very good words for the lips: especially prunes and prism. — Charles Dickens

A *compound verb* consists of two or more verbs having the same subject.

> We are born crying, live complaining, and die disappointed.
> — Thomas Fuller

Conjunction: A single word or group of words that connects other words or groups of words. See Parts of Speech.

Co-ordinate conjunctions connect words, phrases, or clauses of equal rank, e.g., *and, but, or, nor, for, however, moreover, then, therefore, yet, still, both/and, not only/but also, either/or, neither/nor.*

Subordinate conjunctions connect clauses of unequal rank (i.e., an independent and a dependent clause). Examples are *as, as if, because, before, if, since, that, till, unless, when, where, whether.*

Dangling Modifier: A modifier with an unclear reference. See p. 55.

Gerund: The *-ing* form of a verb that serves as a noun.

Seeing is *believing.*

Does anyone object to my *smoking*?

(Note the possessive pronoun; "Does anyone object to *me* smoking?" would be incorrect.)

Infinitive: The form of a verb used with *to.* To eat, to drink, to recover. *Split infinitives* (a word inserted between *to* and the verb) no longer seem to arouse any ire, but they are probably best avoided unless the unsplit form produces ambiguity or clumsiness, or if the message just can't be conveyed as effectively any other way.

The English-speaking world may be divided into (1) those who neither know nor care what a split infinitive is; (2) those who do not know, but care very much; (3) those who know and condemn; (4) those who know and approve; and (5) those who know and distinguish. Those who neither know nor care are the vast majority, and are a happy folk, to be envied by most of the minority classes. — H. W. Fowler

Intransitive Verb: A verb that does not require an object to complete its meaning. A given verb can be either transitive (i.e., requiring an object) or intransitive, depending on its use.

> He met his sister at the airport. (Transitive - *sister* is the object of the verb *met*).

> The delegates met last week. (Intransitive - no object)

Misplaced Modifier: A modifier that gives a misleading meaning by being incorrectly placed in a sentence. See p. 55.

Nonrestrictive Elements: Words, phrases, or clauses that are not essential to the meaning.

Noun: A word that names a person, place, thing, quality or act. See Parts of Speech.

Object: A word or group of words that receives or is affected by the action of a verb.

Participle: A form of a verb which has some of the properties of an adjective and some of a verb. Like an adjective, it can modify a noun or pronoun; like a verb, it can take an object.

> *Hoping* for a good score, I nervously opened the envelope.

Glowing coals, *frayed* collars, *run-down* heels, and *whipped* cream are examples of verb forms that function as adjectives, and thus are participles.

Parts of Speech: Nouns, pronouns, verbs, adjectives, adverbs, prepositions, conjunctions, and interjections. In the days of *McGuffey's Reader*, students used to learn the parts of speech with the help of the following jingle:

> A NOUN's the name of anything,
> As, *school* or *garden, hoop* or *swing.*
>
> ADJECTIVES tell the kind of noun;
> As, *great, small, pretty, white,* or *brown.*
>
> Instead of nouns the PRONOUNS stand:
> *Their* heads, *your* face, *its* paw, *his* hand.
>
> VERBS tell of something being done:
> You *read, count, sing, laugh, jump,* or *run.*
>
> How things are done the ADVERBS tell;
> As, *slowly, quickly, ill,* or *well.*
>
> CONJUNCTIONS join the words together;
> As, men *and* women, wind *or* weather.
>
> The PREPOSITION stands before
> a noun; as, *in* or *through* a door.
>
> The INTERJECTION shows surprise;
> As, *Oh!* how pretty! *Ah!* how wise!

Passive Voice: The form of the verb used when the subject is the receiver of the action. See Rule 70.

Person: Person denotes the speaker (first person), the person spoken to (second person), or the person or thing spoken of (third person).

Possessive: Showing ownership; also known as the genitive case. See Case.

Prefix: A word element which is attached to the front of a root word and changes the meaning of the root: *dis*belief, *in*attentive.

Preposition: A word or group of words that shows the relation between its object and some other word in the sentence. See Parts of Speech.

> Alice gazed *through* the looking glass.

Perhaps no other rule of grammar has prompted so many to say so much as the now-outdated rule prohibiting ending a sentence with a preposition. Here are two comments on the subject:

> *This is the sort of English up with which I will not put.*
> — Winston Churchill

> *The grammar has a rule absurd*
> *Which I would call an outworn myth:*
> *A preposition is a word*
> *You mustn't end a sentence with.*
> — Berton Braley

Pronoun: A word that takes the place of a noun. See Parts of Speech.

Possessive pronouns represent the possessor and the thing possessed: The book is *mine*.

Personal pronouns are *I, you, he, she, it,* and their inflected forms (*me, my, your, them,* etc.).

Relative pronouns (who, which, that, what) join adjective clauses to their antecedents (i.e., what they refer to): The girl *who* sang is here.

Restrictive Elements: Words, phrases, or clauses that are essential to the meaning.

Run-on: The error in which two independent clauses are written as a single sentence, without any conjunction or punctuation separating them.

> The tennis match ended in a tie everyone agreed that it was too late to play a tie-breaker.

This error would be corrected by any of the following: adding a semicolon between the two clauses; making the clauses into separate sentences; or adding a comma and a conjunction between the clauses.

> The tennis match ended in a tie; everyone agreed that it was too late to play a tie-breaker.

> The tennis match ended in a tie. Everyone agreed that it was too late to play a tie-breaker.

> The tennis match ended in a tie, but everyone agreed that it was too late to play a tie-breaker.

Subject: The part of a sentence about which something is said.

> *Time* flies.

Subjective Case: Nominative case. See Case.

Suffix: A word element added to the end of a root or stem word, serving to make a new word or an inflected form of the word: gentle*ness*, mother*hood*, depend*able*, hilari*ous*, end*ed*, child*ren*, walk*ing*.

Transitive Verb: A verb that requires a direct object to complete its meaning. See Intransitive Verb.

Unit Modifier: See Compound Adjective.

Verb: A word that expresses action, being, or occurrence. See Parts of Speech.

Voice: See Active Voice, Passive Voice.

Frequently Misspelled Words

FREQUENTLY MISSPELLED WORDS *

Note: The following list contains several pairs of "sound-alikes." A brief definition identifies the first of the sound-alike words; the second is defined following its alphabetical entry.

A

abacus
aberration
abridgment
abscess
abscissa
absence
accelerator
accept (receive)
   except
accessible
accessory
accommodate
accumulate
achievement
acknowledgment
acquittal
acumen
acupuncture
adjourn
adolescence
advantageous
advertisement
aegis
aerosol
affidavit
aging
algae
algorithm
align
alimony

alkaline
allegiance
allotment
allotted
all right
already
amanuensis
amoeba
amplifier
anachronism
analogous
analysis
ancillary
anesthetic
annihilate
anomaly
anonymous
antihistamine
apartheid
aperture
aphrodisiac
apparatus
apparel
apparent
appraisal
apropos
aqueduct
arctic
arraign
arteriosclerosis
arthritis

ascorbic
asphyxiate
aspirin
assessor
assistance
asterisk
asymmetry
attendance
attorneys
auditor
autumn
auxiliary

B

bachelor
bailiff
balance
ballistic
balloon
ballot
bankruptcy
barbiturate
barrel
basically
beneficiary
benign
bereave
berserk
bifurcate
bigot

*In Canada, the spelling of many words is optional. The use of *our* in words like colour and honour is gradually giving way to *or*, as you will notice in almost every newspaper. Where two spellings are given here, the first one seems to be the more widely used one now, although both are acceptable.

bilateral
bilingual
binary
biodegradable
biopsy
bipartisan
blatant
bloc (group)
bludgeon
bologna
bouillon (soup)
    bullion
bourgeois
boutique
boycott
braille
brief
bruise
budget
bulletin
bullion (gold)
    bouillon
bureaucracy
burglar
business
byte

C

caffeine
calendar
calorie
campaign
cannot
capillary
capitulate
capsule
captain
carafe
carat
carbohydrate
carburetor
Caribbean
carriage

catechism
category
cathode
Caucasian
caucus
caveat
ceiling
cellar
cellophane
Celsius
cemetery
censor
centigrade
centimetre, centimeter
centrifugal
cerebral
certain
cesarean
    (or Caesarean)
chaise longue
champagne
changeable
charisma
chassis
chauvinist
chiropractor
chlorophyll
chocolate
cholesterol
Christian
cipher
circuit
cirrhosis
clone
clothes
coalition
cocaine
coefficient
cognac
coliseum
    (or colosseum)
collar
collateral
colloquial

cologne
colonel
color, colour
colossal
column
commitment
commodities
compatible
competent
computer
condemn
conductor
conduit
conglomerate
conjugal
conscience
consensus
consortium
corps
correspondence
counterfeit
coup d'etat
courtesy
cousin
cryptic
cul-de-sac
culinary
curtain
cybernetics
cylinder

D

database
debit
debugging
decadence
deceive
decibel
deciduous
deductible
defendant
defence, defense
deferred

deficit
depot
depreciate
descend
desiccate
desperate
deterrent
develop
diagnostic
diaphragm
dichotomy
dictionary
diesel
digital
dilemma
dinosaur
director
disappear
disappoint
disburse (pay out)
   disperse
discernible
discreet (cautious)
discrete (separate)
disperse (scatter)
   disburse
dissatisfied
dissipate
distributor
doubt
dyeing (coloring)
dying (death)

E

eccentric
echelon
ecstasy
eighth
either
elevator
elicit (draw forth)
   illicit
embarrass

emphysema
empirical
encyclopedia
endeavor, endeavour
entrepreneur
envelop (surround)
envelope (stationery)
epitome
equipped
equity
equivocal
errata
erratic
erroneous
esoteric
esthetic
   (or aesthetic)
euthanasia
exaggerate
except (other than)
   accept
exhaust
exhibition
exhilarate
existential
exonerate
exorbitant
exponential
extraterrestrial

F

facsimile
factor
Fahrenheit
fallacy
familiar
favor, favour
faze (disturb)
   phase
feasibility
feature
February
fetus

fiduciary
fierce
filibuster
finesse
fission
fluorescent
fluoridate
focused
   (or focussed)
foreign
foreword
forfeit
franchise
freight
fulfill

G

galaxy
gallon
garrulous
genealogy
generic
geriatrics
gestalt
ghetto
governor
graffiti
gram
grammar
grateful
grief
grievance
guarantee
guerilla
guess
gynecology

H

hallucinogen
handkerchief
harass
Hawaiian

height
heinous
heir
hemorrhage
herbicide
heroin (drug)
hertz
hiatus
hierarchy
hirsute
holistic
holocaust
hologram
homogeneous
homonym
honor, honour
hors d'oeuvres
hospice
hydraulic
hygiene
hymn
hypnosis
hypocrisy

I

ideology
idiosyncrasy
idle (inactive)
idol (image)
illicit (forbidden)
   elicit
impermeable
imprimatur
inadvertent
incalculable
incessant
incidentally
incumbent
independent
indictment
indispensable
infrared
innocuous

innuendo
inoculate
insecticide
intermittent
interrupt
intravenous
iridescent
irrelevant
irresistible
irrigate
island

J

janitor
jeopardize
jewellery, jewelry
joule
journey
judgment
junta

K

khaki
kibbutz
kilometre, kilometer
kilowatt
knowledge

L

label
labyrinth
laissez faire
laser
league
legislature
leisure
leukemia
liable
liaison
libel
licence — noun

license — verb
lieutenant
lightning
likable
likelihood
liquefy
liquor
litre, liter
logarithm
logistics
lunar

M

mahogany
maintain
maintenance
malignant
mandatory
manoeuvre
maraschino
margarine
marijuana
   (or marihuana)
marital
marshal
massacre
mathematics
matrix
mayonnaise
mediocre
megabyte
megawatt
memento
menstruation
metaphor
metastasize
metric
microfiche
micrometer
microprocessor
migraine
mileage
milieu

milligram
millimetre, millimeter
minestrone
miniature
minuscule
minutiae
miscellaneous
mischievous
missile
misspell
mnemonic
moccasin
modem
molecular
monaural
monetary
monitor
morass
mortgage
mosquito
mustache
myopia

N

naive
narcissism
necessary
neither
neophyte
nickel
niece
noxious
nozzle
nuance
nuclear

O

obesity
occasion
occurrence
odyssey
ombudsman

omelet
omniscient
ophthalmologist
opiate
orgy
oscillator
overrun

P

panacea
parallel
paralyze
parameter
paraphernalia
paraplegic
parliament
parochial
pasteurized
percolator
per diem
peremptory
perennial
perimeter
peripheral
permissible
perquisite
personnel
perspiration
pertinent
pharmaceutical
phase (aspect)
    faze
Philippines
phosphorus
physician
physics
pinnacle
plebiscite
pneumonia
poisonous
pollutant
polyester
polymer

porcelain
porous
Portuguese
posthumous
potpourri
prairie
precede
precious
preferred
prerogative
prevalent
privilege
procedure
proceed
propeller
prophecy (noun)
prophesy (verb)
protein
protocol
proxy
pseudonym
psychology
ptomaine
publicly

Q

quasi
questionnaire
queue
quiche
quixotic

R

radar
rapport
rarefy
rebuttal
recede
receipt
receive
receptacle
recession

reciprocal
recommend
reconnaissance
recuperate
recurrence
referred
rehearsal
relevant
religious
remembrance
renege
rescind
resistance
restaurant
resuscitate
rhetoric
rheumatism
rhythm
robotics
roentgen
rotor

S

saboteur
saccharin (noun)
sacrilegious
salmon
satellite
savvy
scenario
schedule
scissors
secretary
seizure
separate
sergeant
siege
sieve
silhouette
similar
simulate

simultaneous
sinecure
sinus
siphon
skeptical, sceptical
sophomore
spaghetti
stratagem
strategy
stupefy
subpoena, subpena
subterranean
subtle
succeed
succinct
suffrage
superintendent
supersede
supervisor
surprise
surveillance
syllable
synagogue
synonymous
synopsis
syntax
syphilis

T

tariff
therapy
thief
threshold
tobacco
tongue
toxin
trafficking
tranquilizer
trauma
treasurer

trek
tyranny

U

ubiquitous
umbilical
unanimous
unerring
unnecessary
unprecedented
usage

V

vacillation
vacuum
vehicle
vengeance
verbatim
versatile
veterinarian
vice versa
vicious
vicissitude
villain
visitor

W

waiver
weird
wholly
withheld
womb
woolen

Y

yield

Z

zucchini

Bibliography

Brusaw, C. T., G. J. Alred, W. E. Oliu, *The Business Writer's Handbook*, New York: St. Martin's Press, 1976.

Canadian Press, *Style Book, 1978.*

Corder, Jim W. and Walter S. Avis, *Handbook of Current English,* Canadian ed., Toronto: Gage Educational Publishing Ltd., 1979.

Doris, Lillian and Besse May Miller, *Complete Secretary's Handbook,* 4th ed., revised by Mary A. DeVries, Englewood Cliffs, N. J.: Prentice-Hall, Inc., 1977.

Fowler, H. W., *A Dictionary of Modern English Usage*, London: Oxford University Press, 1926.

Gavin, Ruth E. and William A. Sabin, *Reference Manual for Stenographers and Typists*, 4th ed., New York: Gregg Division/McGraw-Hill Book Co., 1970.

Lanham, Richard A., *Revising Business Prose,* New York: Charles Scribner's Sons, 1981.

Manual of Style, A, 13th ed., Chicago: University of Chicago Press, 1982.

Miller, Casey and Kate Swift, *The Handbook of Nonsexist Writing,* New York; Harper & Row, 1981.

Roman, Kenneth and Joel Raphaelson, *Writing That Works,* New York: Harper & Row. 1981.

Shaw, Harry, *McGraw-Hill Handbook of English,* 3rd Canadian ed., Toronto, McGraw-Hill, 1979.

Strunk, William, Jr., and E. B. White, *The Elements of Style*, 3rd ed., New York: The Macmillan Co., 1979.

Venolia, Jan, *Better Letters: A Handbook of Business and Personal Correspondence,* Berkeley, CA: Ten Speed Press, 1982.

Words into Type, 3rd ed., Englewood Cliffs, N. J.: Prentice Hall, Inc., 1974.

Dictionaries

American Heritage Dictionary of the English Language, The: American Heritage, New York

Funk & Wagnalls Standard College Dictionary: Funk & Wagnalls, Canadian ed., Fitzhenry and Whiteside, Toronto

Gage Canadian Dictionary, The: Gage Educational Publishing Limited, Toronto.

Random House Dictionary of the English Language, The: Random House, New York

Reader's Digest Great Encyclopedic Dictionary, The: Reader's Digest Association, Pleasantville, New York

Webster's Eighth New Collegiate Dictionary: G&C Merriam, Springfield, Mass.
  (the abridged version of *Webster's Third Edition*)

Webster's Third New International Dictionary (unabridged): G&C Merriam, Springfield, Mass.

INDEX

CANADIAN
ORDER FORM
SELF-COUNSEL SERIES

02/85

NATIONAL TITLES:

Adopted?	3.95
Advertising for Small Business	4.95
Assertiveness for Managers	8.95
Basic Accounting	5.95
Be a Better Manager	7.95
Better Book for Getting Hired	9.95
Business Guide to Effective Speaking	6.95
Business Guide to Telephone Systems	7.95
Buying (and Selling) a Small Business	6.95
Changing Your Name in Canada	3.50
Civil Rights	8.95
Collection Techniques for the Small Business	4.95
Complete Guide to Being Your Own Home Contractor	19.95
Credit, Debt, and Bankruptcy	5.95
Criminal Procedure in Canada	12.95
Design Your Own Logo	9.95
Drinking and Driving	4.50
Editing Your Newsletter	14.95
Exporting	12.50
Family Ties That Bind	7.95
Federal Incorporation and Business Guide	12.95
Financial Control for the Small Business	5.95
Financial Freedom on $5 A Day	6.95
For Sale By Owner	4.95
Franchising in Canada	5.95
Fundraising	5.50
Getting Money	14.95
Getting Sales	14.95
Getting Started	11.95
How You Too Can Make a Million . . . In the Mail Order Business	8.95
Immigrating to Canada	12.95
Immigrating to the U.S.A.	14.95
Importing	21.95
Insuring Business Risks	3.50
Learn to Type Fast	6.50
Life Insurance for Canadians	3.50
Managing Your Office Records and Files	14.95
Media Law Handbook	6.50
Mike Grenby's Money Book	5.50
Mike Grenby's Tax Tips	6.95
Money Spinner	14.95
Mortgage and Foreclosure Handbook	5.95
Parents' Guide to Day Care	5.95
Practical Guide to Financial Management	5.95
Resort Condos	4.50
Retirement Guide for Canadians	9.95
Start and Run a Profitable Beauty Salon	14.95
Start and Run a Profitable Consulting Business	
Start and Run a Profitable Craft Business	10.95
Start and Run a Profitable Home Typing Business	9.95
Start and Run a Profitable Restaurant	10.95
Start and Run a Profitable Retail Business	11.95
Start and Run a Profitable Video Store	10.95
Starting a Successful Business in Canada	12.95
Tax Law Handbook	12.95
Taxpayer Alert!	4.95
Tax Shelters	6.95
Trusts and Trust Companies	3.95
Upper Left-Hand Corner	10.95
Using the Access to Information Act	5.95
Word Processing	8.95
Working Couples	5.50
Write Right!	(Cloth) 5.95 / (Paper)

PROVINCIAL TITLES:
Please indicate which provincial edition is required.
Consumer Book
☐B.C. 7.95   ☐Ontario 6.95

Divorce Guide
☐B.C. 10.95   ☐Alberta 9.95   ☐Ontario 9.95   ☐Man./Sask.

Employee/Employer Rights
☐B.C. 6.95   ☐Alberta 6.95   ☐Ontario 5.50

Fight That Ticket
☐B.C. 5.95   ☐Alberta   ☐Ontario 3.95

Incorporation Guide
☐B.C. 14.95   ☐Alberta 14.95   ☐Ontario 14.95   ☐Man./Sask.

Landlord/Tenant Rights
☐B.C.   ☐Alberta 5.50   ☐Ontario 6.95

Marriage & Family Law
☐B.C. 6.95   ☐Alberta 5.95   ☐Ontario 7.95

Probate Guide
☐B.C. 12.95   ☐Alberta 9.95   ☐Ontario 9.95

Real Estate Guide
☐B.C. 7.95   ☐Alberta 4.95   ☐Ontario 6.50

Small Claims Court Guide
☐B.C. 6.95   ☐Alberta   ☐Ontario 5.95

Wills
☐B.G. 5.50   ☐Alberta 5.95   ☐Ontario 5.50

Wills/Probate Procedure
☐Sask./Man. 4.95

PACKAGED FORMS:

Divorce
☐B.C. 12.95   ☐Alberta 12.95   ☐Ontario 14.50   ☐Man. 8.50   ☐Sask. 12.50

Incorporation
☐B.C. 12.95   ☐Alberta 11.95   ☐Ontario 14.95

☐Man. 7.95   ☐Sask. 7.95   ☐Federal 9.95

☐Minute Books 16.50

Probate
☐B.C. Administration 14.95   ☐B.C. Probate 14.95   ☐Alberta 13.95   ☐Ontario 15.50

Sell Your Own Home
☐B.C. 4.95   ☐Alberta 4.95   ☐Ontario 4.95

☐ Rental Form Kit (B.C., Alberta, Ontario, Man./Sask.)   5.95

☐ Have You Made Your Will?   5.95

☐ If You Love Me Put It In Writing   Contract Kit   9.95

☐ If You Leave Me Put It In Writing   B.C. Separation Agreement Kit   14.95

NOTE: *All prices subject to change without notice.*

Books are available in book and department stores, or use the order form below.
Please enclose cheque or money order (plus sales tax where applicable) or give us your
MasterCard or Visa Number (please include validation and expiry date).

(PLEASE PRINT)

Name _____

Address _____

City _____

Province _____ Postal Code _____

☐ Visa/ ☐ MasterCard Number _____

Validation Date _____ Expiry Date _____

If order is under $20.00, add $1.00 for postage and handling.

Please send orders to:

INTERNATIONAL SELF-COUNSEL PRESS LTD.   ☐ Check here for free catalogue.
306 West 25th Street
North Vancouver, British Columbia
V7N 2G1